ANIMAL MEDITATION
PART ONE

TIPS AND EXERCISES TO UNLOCK YOUR MYSTICAL POTENTIAL TO CONNECT WITH YOUR SPIRITUAL ANIMAL GUIDE

ADESH SILVA

© **Copyright 2020 - All rights reserved.**

The content contained within this book may not be reproduced, duplicated or transmitted without direct written permission from the author or the publisher.

Under no circumstances will any blame or legal responsibility be held against the publisher, or author, for any damages, reparation, or monetary loss due to the information contained within this book, either directly or indirectly.

Legal Notice:

This book is copyright protected. It is only for personal use. You cannot amend, distribute, sell, use, quote or paraphrase any part, or the content within this book, without the consent of the author or publisher.

Disclaimer Notice:

Please note the information contained within this document is for educational and entertainment purposes only. All effort has been executed to present accurate, up to date, reliable, complete information. No warranties of any kind are declared or implied. Readers acknowledge that the author is not engaged in the rendering of legal, financial, medical or professional advice. The content within this book has been derived from various sources. Please consult a licensed professional before attempting any techniques outlined in this book.

By reading this document, the reader agrees that under no circumstances is the author responsible for any losses, direct or indirect, that are incurred as a result of the use of the information contained within this document, including, but not limited to, errors, omissions, or inaccuracies.

CONTENTS

Introduction 7

1. AN INTRODUCTION TO LAND SPIRIT ANIMALS 13
   Aardvarks 13
   Alpacas 14
   Alligators 14
   Ants 14
   Antelope 14
   Apes 15
   Armadillos 15
   Baboons 15
   Badgers 16
   Bears 16
   Beavers 17
   Bighorn Sheep 17
   Bison 17
   Black Panthers 18
   Boars 18
   Bobcats 18
   Bulls 19
   Bushbabies 19
   Camels 19
   Cats 19
   Cheetahs 20
   Chimpanzees 21
   Chinchillas 21
   Chipmunks 21

Cougars	21
Cows	22
Coyotes	22
Deer	22
Dingoes	23
Dogs	23
Donkeys	24
Elephants	24
Elks	25
Foxes	25
Gazelles	25
Giraffes	26
Goats	26
Gophers	26
Gorillas	26
Groundhogs	27
Hares	27
Hedgehogs	27
Hippopotami	27
Horses	28
Hyenas	28
Jackals	28
Jaguars	29
Kangaroos	29
Koalas	29
Lemmings	29
Lemurs	30
Leopards	30
Lions	30
Llamas	31
Lynx	31
Marmosets	31
Minks	31

Moles	32
Mongoose	32
Monkeys	32
Moose	33
Mountain Goats	33
Mice	33
Mules	33
Musk Oxen	34
Muskrats	34
Opossums	34
Ocelots	35
Orangutans	35
Oryx	35
Otters	35
Oxen	36
Pandas	36
Pigs	36
Platypus	37
Porcupines	37
Possums	37
Rabbits	37
Raccoons	38
Rams	38
Rats	38
Rhinoceros	38
Sheep	39
Shrews	39
Skunks	39
Sloths	39
Snakes	40
Squirrels	40
Tapirs	41
Tigers	41

Warthogs	41
Weasels	42
Wolves	42
Zebras	43

2. HOW TO CHOOSE THE BEST LAND ANIMAL FOR YOU — 44
Connecting to Spirit Animals — 45
Strengthening the Bond — 48

3. WHAT DOES IT MEAN WHEN SPIRIT ANIMALS APPEAR TO YOU? — 52
How They Appear — 52
Translations — 56

4. GUIDED SESSION FOR INITIAL CONNECTION — 60
Calling Your Spirit Animal — 61

5. GUIDED SESSION FOR SELF-IMPROVEMENT — 66
Horsing Spirits — 66

6. GUIDED SESSION TO HEAL FROM PAST TRAUMA — 72
Slithering Rejuvenation — 73

7. GUIDED SESSION FOR A DEEPER PURPOSE — 78
A Welcomed Companion — 78

Conclusion — 85
References — 89

INTRODUCTION

Pythagoras once said: "Animals share with us the privilege of having a soul." There's no deeper connection you can possess than that of a soul. You have a human soulmate, but you don't realize that there are incredible beasts connected to your deepest desires, passions, pains, and spiritual essence. They walk this earth with you, and they'll activate the soulmate bond when you need it the most.

I once stood at a crossroads before I started working. I was fresh out of college when I got my dog. My life was budding with choices as many young adults face. On this day, by some accident I had two job interviews scheduled at the same time. It could've been due to my excitement and sheer eagerness to get into the workforce but in the end I had to choose between the two equally desirable companies. Unfor-

INTRODUCTION

tunately, leading up to this interview was a sad display of poor time management.

The shirt I had decided to wear that day was wrinkled, and I had no time left to iron it. I ironed just the front part and put my nicest coat on over it to cover my shabby work. I owned two ties, and that was where things began to get weird. Color schemes didn't matter too much to me, and a clever idea had popped into my mind. My tie should decide which interview I attend, blue stripes or orange ducks. What else is there to do at still a young age when options are so limited? I stood in front of the mirror with a tie in each hand and resorted to delegating the choice to a game of 'eenie-meenie-miney-mo.' Suddenly, my four-legged friend jumped up, ripping the orange tie from my hand and tore it to shreds. That settled it. He made the choice for me that day, and nearly a decade later, I have made it to the top ranks of a huge corporate empire.

This story of how I chose the interview that changed my life isn't as strange or careless as it sounds. Native Americans, shamans, and other ancient cultures have been known to rely on the soul connections they share with their spirit guides to show them the right path. My dog allowed me to get where I am today, and your spirit animal guides can do the same. It doesn't matter if you're trying to rid yourself of emotional chains or pursue the best version of yourself. You might lead a mindful life and visit Reiki practitioners to alleviate troublesome energy from your body; however, you can also open your mind to the creatures that share a soul with you.

Dogs aren't just pets, and tigers aren't just zoo attractions. Every animal has a boundless source of spiritual energy they'd love to share with humanity. Hindus and shamans have always been able to connect to the spiritual world through the essence of animals, and Native American tribes used animal guides as totems to open their worlds to every possibility (Beauchesne, 2018). The chieftains of these tribes understood the bond we share with animals, and they used this connection to find deeper meaning in their lives. Animal spirits can bring you a deeper purpose, help you deal with painful memories, and guide through you on to a path where everything becomes possible.

Some animal spirits offer healing energy, and others share their characteristic strengths with you. Animals naturally have a strong bond with the spiritual world, and can see more in-depth than you or I. You can connect with animal spirits that allow you to use their spiritual vision to see what lies ahead, and find real power in this bond. There is also a group of spirits that operates in the shadows. You might not know that you're bonded to them, but they can feel your essence and energy shifts.

INTRODUCTION

How many times have you encountered the same animal by accident more than a few times? Where you aren't even in the right environment for that specific animal, but it happens anyway. Spirit animals know when they are required and will start appearing to us. This can be in our dreams and in less subtle visitations. Medicine men from native tribes would communicate with spirit animals because they act as a bridge from this world to the spirit realm thus enabling them to find answers for pain. You can spread your wings and become more than who you are now. The beauty is that the connection between you and your animal is as unique as fingerprints. You don't need to be a shaman to become one with your spirit animal.

Life isn't always as we picture, but you can change this by allowing your spirit animal to guide you. Each one has a unique set of strengths that can push you closer to the life you desire. If only you knew earlier in life that denying this bond could hold you back from greatness. You never knew that you could possess the power of a bear, the agility of a cheetah, and the curiosity of a monkey. Imagine what these characteristics could do for you. Today, I have more than I ever dreamed. I have a wonderful family that practices a mindful and holistic lifestyle with me. My passion for self-growth becomes deeper by the day, and I would love for my children to grow into the best versions of themselves. You can have all of this by learning everything there is to know about your spirit animal.

I've spent years harnessing the power of my spirit guides after realizing how things could've been different if my first roommate didn't guide me to become the successful man I am today. I've learned so much, and my passion can only be shared with someone at a crossroads now. Are you ready to learn about some incredible land spirit animals and how to connect with them, deepening the bond? This connection is only possible through higher consciousness, and you'll have four guided sessions here to help you communicate with your spirit animal. I only have one question for you. How much do you really want to connect your soul to these spirits that walk among us?

1

AN INTRODUCTION TO LAND SPIRIT ANIMALS

Land spirit animals are intuitive and bring about a more profound sense of awareness. They help us remain grounded, physically and mentally. Each one is a phenomenal creature that connects with you in their special way. There are many land animals to guide you, heal you, and help you reach the goals you want. You must understand the characteristics of each one to harness their strengths and connect with them.

AARDVARKS

The aardvark or anteater symbolizes emotional stability, insight, a keen sense of danger, and the ability to be happy in solitude. It guides you to follow your instincts and remain cautious before entering relationships or new jobs.

ALPACAS

Alpacas are temperamental and strong-spirited animals. They don't tame for companionship easily, but they exude self-preservation. Alpacas are hardy animals, and they're capable of adapting to changes.

ALLIGATORS

Alligators love taking things slowly and thinking everything through. They're territorial and protective creatures. Alligators would never allow anyone to step over their boundaries. The defensive alligator is often called upon when you need to rise out of a difficult period in life.

ANTS

Ants can carry so much on their tiny shoulders. They don't procrastinate and have faith in reaching their desires.

ANTELOPE

Antelope are highly adaptable, evasive, and exhibit a keen survival instinct. They're also mentally adaptable, always finding a way to overcome obstacles. However, every plan is strategic.

APES

Apes use their vocal expressions and add physical gestures to make communication more powerful. They're also wise, curious, imaginative, inspiring, and loyal. Apes show strong leadership while remaining compassionate and dignified. Apes are also nurturing and easy to connect with.

ARMADILLOS

Armadillos carry self-preservation on their shoulders. They also respect and understand boundaries. They demand respect for their boundaries too. Armadillos are discerning creatures, and they make sure that everyone knows exactly what they want.

BABOONS

Baboons are mediating counselors that help you down the right path to the afterlife. It's a divine and majestic animal. Baboon excrements were even used in aphrodisiacs at one point, so their sexual prowess is high. They represent old-school values, family, and judgment.

BADGERS

Badgers are persistent animals that keep stories. They have earthly wisdom and surprising courage for their size. Badgers know how to protect themselves aggressively against insurmountable challenges.

BEARS

Bears are the first of the great spirit animals and are revered by humans before any other animal. Shamans often encounter the spirit of this beast, but it isn't unusual for regular meditators to harness them. Bears are highly-protective, especially of their young, and one of the most dangerous wood creatures; we can learn discipline from them. Gathering your needs and storing them for hibernation is a disciplined quality.

Bears are wiser than we give them credit for. They tend to understand life and what they're capable of. They set boundaries and practice reflection before jumping into a problem. Their strength is also emotional, but they treat their young with gentleness. Each bear type has some additional spirit essence.

The black bear is shy, secretive, and loves its solitude.

Brown bears are curious and fair leaders.

The grizzly bear is a stable, tenacious, and introspective healer. It resonates with power, maturity, and leadership, but it never loses self-control.

Polar bears are mystical animals that shamans use as a dream guide. They're wise, fearless, intelligent, and powerful. Polar bears are great swimmers, and this represents being able to move through emotional waters with ease.

BEAVERS

Beavers are the most popular spirit animal in Canada. They're skillful masters and believe in building dreams. They don't procrastinate but rather engineer a productive way forward. Beavers are durable, emotionally stable, and lead a structured life.

BIGHORN SHEEP

Bighorn sheep or battering rams are assertive, defensive, and agile as heck. They represent new beginnings and powerful moves forward by being creative and durable.

BISON

Bison or buffalo are sacred and prosperous beings with earthly knowledge and character strength that a free spirit needs. Buffalo will sacrifice themselves for another. They teach gratitude and grounding. The rare white buffalo symbolizes feminine courage, nurturing, and prophetic knowledge.

BLACK PANTHERS

Black panthers are a name used for brown or black wild cats. They're magical and nocturnal, and they hold other-worldly knowledge to find light in the dark. They have keen insight into others, hold a sexual mystery about them, and hide their emotions.

BOARS

Boars or wild hogs are famous for turning weakness into a strength. They face fears and are emotionally strong. Boars possess bravery and nobility in a masculine style that guides you to be honest with yourself.

BOBCATS

Bobcats are natural hunters that utilize stealth, patience, and perseverance. They symbolize patience, and show you how to avoid people you don't need in your life. Bobcats reflect and gather strength before an attack.

BULLS

Bulls are sacrificial animals that pride themselves in offering nourishment to people. They're strong animals that offer insight and are protective of their calves. Bulls and steers have one thing in common in the fact that they provide.

Steers have an undying desire to fertilize thoughts, possessions, and ideas. They also have tenacity and stability.

BUSHBABIES

Bushbabies or night monkeys are nocturnal animals that strive for agility and adaptability to new surroundings.

CAMELS

Camels have an unwavering ability to remain positive in the face of doubt, uncertainty, and hard times. They cross deserts while persevering until they reach the next oasis.

CATS

Cats, feral or domesticated, have a deep spirituality as they only live in the present moment. They've always been magical and mysterious. Cats are agile in mind and body while being unpredictable, independent, and curious.

They're brave as they often face their fears in the dark. Even though you can't own a cat as they own you instead, their energy calms yours down when you feel emotional. Cats are guardians of the sacred worlds with a strong connection between the spirit world and ours. Different cats have varying characteristics.

Kittens are innocent and helpless, whereas feral cats teach us to be cautious of those around us. Barn cats are semi-feral too. Black cats are ritualistic and could guide intuitive dreams. Calico cats are femininely mysterious, and Manx cats are highly intelligent. Munchkins are resilient cats because you'd think their short legs prevent agility, but it doesn't. Siamese cats are affectionate but demanding, and sphinx cats represent youthfulness. White cats are healing spirits because they represent the truth about the sun if you metaphorically allow yourself to burn without looking after your skin.

CHEETAHS

Cheetahs are agile, swift, and have eyesight you can only wish for. They also focus intently and practice self-care when stressed. Cheetahs are fast animals and will help you keep your eyes on your goals.

CHIMPANZEES

Chimpanzees are intelligent and inventive animals. They understand language and the complexity of modern society. They're also temperamental and protective of their boundaries.

CHINCHILLAS

Chinchillas are effective communicators that love exploring from a distance. Chinchillas are omens, and you should pay attention to what they teach you. They prefer balance and external perceptions.

CHIPMUNKS

Chipmunks are the curious and inquisitive messengers of many realms. Stubborn is another way to describe them. Often, their curiosity sends them chasing their tails. Its presence could indicate recklessness in your life.

COUGARS

Cougars, mountain lions, or pumas are spiritual animals that share the mind, body, and spirit connection. They're also stealthy and patient while leading gracefully. They'll never abuse their power and believe in honest leadership.

COWS

Cows are similar to bulls, but they also represent reproduction and fertility. They are maternal animals that welcome duties and will sacrifice themselves for higher meaning.

COYOTES

Coyotes are naughty but wise animals. Sometimes, the tricks played by a coyote have greater meaning intended for growth and change. Being playful and thoughtful at the same time is a masterful skill. Coyotes make great long-term companions, even if they encourage sacredness.

DEER

Deer show an unwavering understanding of emotions. They represent the connection between the spiritual and the body, or the heart and soul. Deer are capable of encouraging you gently. Male and female deer are graceful, but there are subtle differences between the stag and hind. Hinds are maternal, subtle, and exude femininity. They also resonate with love, compassion, and good intentions. Celts and

American Indians believed that the hind was a symbol for unconditional love (Spirit Walk Ministry, n.d.). Stags are the masculine representations of regeneration and healing again.

DINGOES

Dingoes are Australian wild dogs famous for facing hard times and looking for ways to persecute those who wronged them. They're loyal pack animals and look after their own kind.

DOGS

Dogs represent trust, loyalty, reliability, and protection. They are guardians of people who can't protect themselves and sacred places. Dogs also symbolize friendship and love. Feral dogs represent the return to our previous form when they reenter the wild. Puppies signify devotion and loyalty to people and objects. Beagles are sympathetic, and black dogs offer us guidance to safety. Bulldogs are persistent and tenacious, whereas chihuahuas represent dynamite in small packages. Collies are deeply faithful and spiritual, but dalmatians love exploring. Dalmatians also represent knowledge about the difference between right and wrong.

German shepherds are helpful and obedient, whereas greyhounds are vigilant, agile, and courageous. Huskies have the inner strength to guide you and work great in a team. Mastiffs are persistent dogs that get what they want. Poodles represent expectations and grace, but retrievers have a keen focus on what they want. Saint Bernards make great companions and offer spiritual guidance. Sheepdogs are slightly selfish because they want a group to stick together for their own needs. Terriers are focused on what they want, and whippets might be nervous dogs, but they teach you how to deal with nervousness. White dogs symbolize purity, a lust for life, and renewal.

DONKEYS

Donkeys are versatile, hard-working, determined, and as stubborn as a mule—pun intended. They're also creative, willing, responsible, and dedicated to the spiritual world. They carry your burdens.

ELEPHANTS

Elephants are obedient to their spiritual existence, leadership, and guidance, making them great role models. Never underestimate an elephant because it's a strong animal that will pursue its desires. They listen to everyone around them and have the best memory in the animal kingdom. Elephants can even express emotions, but they don't respond to insults. They're peaceful while remaining aware.

ELKS

Elks are wise, beautiful, proud, and strong animals. They have undying stamina, but they're unpredictable and mysterious. They change from passive to aggressive in the blink of an eye. They have strong observation skills to detect danger.

FOXES

Foxes are globally sacred animals. They're cunning, stealthy, and have shapeshifting protection. Foxes are sacred because they live between dusk and dawn, which is also thought to be the entry point into the spiritual world. Their intelligence is often misunderstood, but they represent the healing of the body, mind, and spirit. The arctic fox is a chancer, but its evolving coat helps it vanish again. The gray fox is a camouflage master and indicates good luck. The red fox is additionally creative and sexual.

GAZELLES

Gazelles are fast, graceful, and agile. They have focused awareness of their environment and have a masterful ability to maneuver.

GIRAFFES

Giraffes are known to have foresight because they can see something coming before anyone else does. They also connect the ground to the spiritual world by walking tall and having their feet dug firmly.

GOATS

Goats are willing to work their way to the top with willingness. They're aware of everything, but they also represent anxiousness, pessimism, and laziness. Seeing one in your dreams could mean you're anxious or pessimistic.

GOPHERS

Gophers look beneath the surface for answers when there are none in plain sight.

GORILLAS

Gorillas are powerful and wise but compassionate. They carry inner sadness or an emotional self. Gorillas keep the peace by being aggressive.

GROUNDHOGS

Groundhogs teach us how to lay low during hard times and understand changes. They are symbolic dream visitors.

HARES

Hares are larger than rabbits, and they possess different symbols. Hares are solitary creatures, but they're tough as nails. Their independence, competitiveness, prowess, and observation are running at full steam. Hares represent ambitions, virtues, and fitness. Jackrabbits are focused, intelligent, witty, and peaceful. Unfortunately, jackrabbits are mischievous and will resort to trickery to get out of a tight spot. They represent chaos.

HEDGEHOGS

Hedgehogs are wise and non-aggressive protectors. They pay close attention to the earth and know its secrets. They prefer to avoid chaos and protect the truth.

HIPPOPOTAMI

The hippopotamus is an honest animal that seeks truth under the surface. They demand respect for the truth and will act intuitively and practically.

HORSES

Horses symbolize freedom and power. They offer you mobility, speed, and adventure. Their power must never be used negatively because of their rebellious and spirited nature. Horses are independent, but they also enjoy companionship. Ponies symbolize magic and make dreams come true.

HYENAS

Hyenas are strange spirit animals. They allow others to kill for them and then pick up the leftovers. However, their strength is that they can laugh at nearly anything. Emotions don't shake them much.

JACKALS

Jackals love protecting the family in companionships. They seem predatory, but their best attribute is that they stick together.

JAGUARS

Jaguars are powerful and aggressive animals capable of multitasking. They're fearless and don't allow chaos to consume them. They can facilitate spiritual connections but are keenly independent. They're also shapeshifters that desire self-empowerment.

KANGAROOS

Kangaroos are calm creatures by nature until a threat springs them. They're protective of their young and capable of leaping from bad situations. These animals always move forward and never look back.

KOALAS

Koalas are unique slow-movers that overcome gradually while being capable of showing empathy. Koalas are the embodiment of positive laziness because they practice self-care and appreciation.

LEMMINGS

Lemmings teach free-thinking and the utilization of available resources. Lemmings guide us to balance our free time with others.

LEMURS

Lemurs are spirits of the night in the forest. They can access knowledge and view the unseen. They have a good understanding of life and are proud of their individuality.

LEOPARDS

Leopards are aggressive, powerful, stealthy, and can communicate with the spirit world. Leopards can gracefully leap over their obstacles and are master environmental negotiators.

LIONS

Lions symbolize the sun and all its energy. They know how to work in a team and respect everyone. Jealousy and anger can't shake them, and they don't allow unnecessary confrontation to sway them. Lions are nurturing and patient. Females are the hunters, and males are the protectors.

LLAMAS

Llamas can carry the weight of the world in their embodiments. They're curious, adaptable, perseverant, and intelligent. Don't underestimate their stubbornness either. Llamas don't take risks and can endure a lot.

LYNX

A lynx sees more than the average eye does. It understands mystery, has knowledge we don't have, and disguises itself easily. The lynx is known to manipulate time and space and can seduce mates with its eyes.

MARMOSETS

Marmosets are agile and don't allow anything to prevent them from reaching their destination. They know to go where they need to before focusing on their desires. They're speedy multi-taskers.

MINKS

Minks are flexible, complex, and philosophical. Their ingenious gracefulness makes them thrive in higher-quality lives. They don't do well in poor circumstances.

MOLES

Moles are solitary guardians of the worlds beneath the surface. They understand energy, knowledge, and hidden treasures. The marsupial mole is wise and never doubts. The shrew mole is capable of finding light in the darkness.

MONGOOSE

The mongoose might look placid, but it's a brave animal. A mongoose is so protective that they'd risk their lives to save a companion. They can also build resistance to the poisons of other creatures. Mongoose also resonates with lustrous energy.

MONKEYS

Monkeys are stable yet unpredictable, curious, swift, agile, and capable of invisibility. Using a monkey's shapeshifting qualities can help us explore different versions of ourselves and choose who we want to be. Be careful about what you choose because monkeys can manifest any desires. The civet is a sexual and nocturnal monkey. The snow monkey is far more resilient and intelligent than its counterparts. Vervet monkeys can be destructive or competitive, so they try to avoid conflict because forgiving and forgetting is better than death.

MOOSE

The moose reflects on its truths. It's majestic, wise, and keeps emotions under control.

MOUNTAIN GOATS

Mountain goats are sturdy creatures that seek higher rewards without feeling guilty.

MICE

Mice are invincible and wise as they go about doing their thing without attracting attention. They obsessively focus on the larger picture and never overlook the obvious.

MULES

Mules are much like donkeys in their stubbornness, but they're intelligent and don't frighten easily.

MUSK OXEN

The musk ox is a resilient animal that can survive just about anything. It defends the vulnerable and doesn't judge adversity.

MUSKRATS

Muskrats can traverse emotional waters and return unscathed. They're adaptable and resourceful, but they're also vicious, cunning, and stealthy.

OPOSSUMS

North American opossums are protective guardians intended to help spiritual seekers reach their spirituality. Opossums are colonizing animals that focus on survival and flexibility. It's a placid creature until it's threatened. Then the claws and teeth show its cunning edge. Opossums play dead because they use strategic shapeshifting to overcome challenges. These animals aren't always what they seem, and life might be throwing you a misunderstood curveball if you see one.

OCELOTS

Ocelots are capable of being in two places at once and can even regenerate themselves in solitude. They're great healing spirits while you need a straight head to figure things out.

ORANGUTANS

Orangutans are gentle, secretive, ingenious, and have certain gracefulness about them. They focus on the details of everything.

ORYX

The oryx has a calm and patient demeanor that doesn't allow anything to sink its ship.

OTTERS

Otters live balanced lives and exude playfulness. They know how to let go of things and allow destiny to guide them.

OXEN

Oxen are also resilient creatures as they were trained to carry the burden of man. They even sacrificed their reproductive organs to serve us. They're persistent, tranquil, caring, rational, positive, and can learn easily.

PANDAS

Pandas enjoy solidarity and move slowly. They love companionship by a mate but want their independence respected as well. However, they eat what they can't digest. They take on challenges they won't overcome. They aren't adaptable and can't always face down an opponent. Pandas are gentle giants. The giant panda is a sacred animal that symbolizes peace and knowledge that's older than saber-tooth tigers.

Red pandas are introverted, but they're content. They're divine creatures that regenerate themselves in solitude.

PIGS

Pigs are one of the most intelligent land animals and respond swiftly. They're dependable, punctual, and love routines. Trusted companionship is required, and pigs can offer healing guidance.

PLATYPUS

The platypus resonates with feminine energy combined with earth and water. It balances a work and play lifestyle. It doesn't know aggression and would never confront another animal.

PORCUPINES

Porcupines represent a child-like nature. However, don't underestimate their strength and agility. They're nocturnal, solitary, and defensive foragers. They teach us how to protect our inner selves with our external defenses.

POSSUMS

Possums from Australia are cunning, aggressive, and defensive, but they're also known as a good omen. The brushtail possum is the healer, and the flying possum is the adventurous one that soars. The pygmy possum is inquisitive and social, whereas the ringtail possum is territorial and social.

RABBITS

Rabbits are intuitive messengers that live in colonies and reproduce easily. They're active during dusk and dawn and could lead you to a shadow spirit realm. Be careful, though, because rabbits manifest negative thoughts as fast as they procreate. It's an opportunistic animal that leaps from one task to another.

RACCOONS

Raccoons are disguise masters that hold various masks for opportunity, cautiousness, secrecy, and transformation.

RAMS

Rams are curious, opportunistic, forward-moving, and imaginative. Rams possess the urge to keep the life force strong.

RATS

Rats are restless, witty, hard-working, and slippery scavengers. They're also shrewd, cunning, and success-driven. Rats are somewhat invisible and can reproduce quickly too.

RHINOCEROS

Rhinoceros are giant survivors that offer power and the ability to be passive and aggressive as required. Rhinos love being alone and are content with their own company, but they bring ancient wisdom and insight.

SHEEP

Sheep are comfortable within their herd. It's a sensitive animal that needs protection. However, sheep are easily influenced.

SHREWS

Small and mole-like, shrews are tenacious and sly animals that often finish things others can't. Shrews can be vindictive, but they can also bring wealth.

SKUNKS

Skunks must never be ignored either because their white stripe represents creative energy that manifests dreams. They're fearless but peaceful if unthreatened. Skunks are loving animals when they overcome their fears.

SLOTHS

Sloths are also positively lazy but wise. Their psychic embodiment is powerful because they soak up every detail around them. Sloths can also stay immersed in emotional waters and swim easily. They're a little rebellious when you threaten their independence.

SNAKES

Snakes are great spirit animals to encounter, and they're capable of healing, transformation, and deeper grounding as they're intricately connected to the earth below. They can also be cunning and sly, but these characteristics are the same as any animal that needs to survive.

SQUIRRELS

Squirrels are gatherers, and that gives them foresight. They prepare emotionally and physically for the future. They can over or under prepare as well, but they're playful creatures. They're capable of tapping into reserved energy and keeping their lives balanced. Gray squirrels don't hibernate and are extremely enthusiastic. Red squirrels are social but assertive and aggressive. Flying squirrels are adaptable to communities during bad times and live in solitude during good times.

TAPIRS

Tapirs are peaceful by nature, and they love wandering along the path less taken. They can be defensive and vicious when threatened, but violence always comes as a last resort.

TIGERS

Tigers symbolize the present moment. It's a nocturnal, passionate, powerful, and adventurous feminine energy. They use inner strength and have the determination to find opportunities. The white tiger seeks personal truth and conviction. It walks the shadows and light. The red tiger represents the summer and fire. The black tiger symbolizes winter and water. The blue tiger is all about spring and vegetation, while the white tiger covers autumn and metal. The yellow tiger controls the earth and all the energy it possesses.

WARTHOGS

Warthogs are vigilant and defensive. They'll even attack a larger animal; however, they seek truth and can't stand disappointment. They're resilient in hot climates but use mud baths to protect their skin.

WEASELS

Weasels know how to find the deeper meaning behind something. They learn to hear their inner voice even if they don't follow the truth of it. Ermine weasels believe in justice and are obsessed with their hygiene. They're brave in battle and compassionate at home. Ferrets are focused, intuitive, and observative. They find secrets, and they're curious, gentle, and opportunistic. Fisher cat weasels are independent and don't allow anyone to manipulate them. Polecat weasels are defensive, boastful, and stand up for their rights. They'll fight back and confront fear. The Siberian weasel is opportunistic, sly, and efficient. They move fast and enjoy the finer side of life. They're intelligent and often reflect on the rewards they earn.

WOLVES

Wolves are also great spiritual beasts. They know how to harness their inner self, and their knowledge and intuition are unmatched. They have hidden secrets and talents which often come out at night. They love being social and mate for life. Their family is prioritized, and they deal with birth and death in the most dignified manner. Wolves are courageous, intelligent, skilled, and witty. They guide you through dreams and meditation while allowing you to see the unseen and change what needs to be changed.

The arctic wolf has the power to manifest dreams and is keenly determined. It can withstand many challenges and always comes out stronger. The white arctic wolf is capable of teaching you how to overcome vulnerability. The gray wolf is the shapeshifter that can regenerate and adapt to anything. It's a mystical guardian. The red wolf shows compassion and innocence. It can help you transform the changes you need.

ZEBRAS

Zebras see everything as black and white, but they can easily become confused and rather see countless grey lines in between. They require delicate balance and are indecisive and emotionally unstable without it.

2

HOW TO CHOOSE THE BEST LAND ANIMAL FOR YOU

There's plenty of confusion around spirit animals as it is generally shrouded in myth and legend. It's easy to envy others who claim to walk with a wolf or feel the essence of a bear, and not understand why you don't possess this beast's spirit inside. Remember, we, too, are animals. We live on the same plane, share the same air, and our bodies return to the same ground when we die. Our spirits enter the same realms as our animal counterparts. Humankind is an animal species, and we already have a connection, it is up to you to develop this meaningful relationship in time.

CONNECTING TO SPIRIT ANIMALS

Have you ever admitted to someone as being strictly a cat or dog person? You do this because you already have a subconscious connection to the animal. That's why you prefer one species to another, even in larger creatures. The world is truly beautiful and bountiful as we have so many choices of spirit guides that embody animals. We start our quest by understanding the connections we've already overlooked. People even prefer specific dog types. Do you love the agility a greyhound possesses, or do you prefer the small prance of the poodle? Start searching for your spirit guide by reflecting on the animals you feel most drawn to.

You're instructed by one rule when it comes to choosing spirit animals. They choose you, and you don't formally decide which one stands by your side. Familiar and similar spirits are drawn to each other. You love horses, and your characteristics are similar. A horse's spirit feels this, and you become bonded to them as a rider. The two of you work together like the earth and the moon. The earth would lose its gravitational orbit if the moon had to disappear. Understand that the dog who lies at your feet like a loyal servant is your spirit guide. You've already been developing a relationship with them.

One reason why spirit animals connect to or choose you is that your characteristics are in tune with each other. The entire world vibrates with varying frequencies, and you'll be better suited to animals that resonate with the same energy as you as long as you have the characteristics of the beast. Most of us have one power animal spirit. Mine might be a bear, and yours might be the cougar, depending on which one has walked the longest with us. Our spirit guides never disappear, but they become less bonded to us if we don't develop the relationship.

They watch us from afar but will always be there when we call upon them. Someone might be sensitive and show compassion to other people, even when it saddens them more. They prioritize others and express aggression when their emotions become too much. This person could be bonded with a gorilla. One way of knowing what spirits are walking near is to understand how they try to appear to you. How often do you see a gorilla in your dreams? Do you see symbols of one often? Maybe you were given a gorilla keychain, saw a news article about one in captivity, and then dreamt of one. These are signs that you want to bond with them.

We need to open our eyes to the spirit animal bondage. We must intentionally call upon them and desire their characteristics to strengthen our own. Also, don't limit yourself to animals you see in your immediate environment; you might bond with a kangaroo who reside mainly in Australia. It will still guide you even though you can't keep it as a pet. You can't keep wolves, bears, and gorillas as pets either. Be open-minded and welcome your spirit guide mindfully through focus and intention. You would've noticed how many of these beautiful beasts have a keen focus because it's a primal trait most of us possess. Connecting to your spirit guide in meditation is one of the easiest ways to communicate with them.

Think about animals you've encountered and use an alternate state of consciousness to call upon them. Many spirit animals can visit you physically too. Normally, if you see an animal that behaves irregularly, and you run into them multiple times in a short period, it means that they're trying to connect with you. Stop complaining about the raccoon that raids your trash and instead notice how it looks at you when in view. Pay attention next time and reflect on how easy you feel during this stare-down. Go into the woods or take a drive to a local park. Use meditation to enter your lower level of consciousness and interact with the animals.

You can also have more than one spirit animal. We generally have one power spirit animal, but you can have seven or 20 spirit animals. Remember to remain mindfully present and observe nature around you to see signs of spirit animals.

Give them attention when they make themselves known. You can also meditate with the direct intention of a specific animal you've seen recently. Cycle through each one's characteristics and determine which spirit guide could help you strengthen a trait you already possess. Some of them can also teach you new habits if you develop a long relationship with them.

Learn more about each animal that interests you because you'll be attracted to animals that suit your personality and inner power. Everyone has character strengths, and spirit guides will help us empower them. Remember to reflect on your interaction with each animal. Compare your animal's characteristics to your personality and think about times these strengths have been useful in your life. Finally, anyone who needs emotional healing or the inner strength to pursue a better life should consider how they can connect to animals with healing or rejuvenating powers. Chances are that one of the animals that chose you already knew what you needed, and they can give it to you.

STRENGTHENING THE BOND

If you're into holistic healing and living spiritually, you're familiar with crystals. Crystals also vibrate with certain energy frequencies, and this can help you develop a stronger relationship with your spirit animal (Sage Goddess, 2017).

ANIMAL MEDITATION PART ONE

Spirit animals might even present themselves to you in the form of gemstones or crystals. So, be aware and attentive, or use these energies to turn a spirit animal into the closest friend you have.

The territorial and wise alligator responds well to skeletal quartz, whereas the mighty ant likes ametrine or dumortierite. Armadillos resonate well with black tourmaline, and the badger is as vibrant as the red amethyst. Powerful bears respond to howlite crystals, and hard-working, team-orientated beavers prefer bismuth. The prosperous boar connects to mahogany obsidian, and the abundance grounding buffalo reacts to turquoise.

Magical and independent cats resonate with carnelians, and the content, community-orientated cow loves zebra jasper or dravite. The gentle, agile, and understanding deer prefer sapphire or hawk's eye, and loyal, protective dogs respond well to hematite. The humble and patient donkey likes red jasper, and the memorable elephant prefers kunzite. The ingeniously cunning fox vibrates best to super seven, and the willing goat bonds well with turquoise. You can connect to the gentle but noble gorilla with lazulite and use Atlantisite to bond with the tenacious groundhog.

Protective hedgehogs might be intrigued by obsidian and lava stone, whereas the intuitive, protective hippopotamus will bond with aquamarine or aqua aura quartz. Adventurous and free-spirited horses will love crazy lace agate or peridot, and psychic jaguars will vibrate to rutilated quartz. The leopard's inner power prefers red and blue aventurine, and the leading lion bonds nicely to sunstone or charoite. The grounded mole prefers star ruby, and the trickster monkey loves topaz and basalt.

The sacred moose spirit attaches itself to dioptase, and the stealthy mouse prefers galena or faden quartz. The Australian possum vibrates with phenacite and playful otters like creedite or fluorite. Gentle pandas resonate with aragonite, and ferocious panthers connect to carnelians. The resourceful pig likes sodalite and idocrase, whereas the balanced platypus prefers tektite. Durable polar bears vibrate to sugilite and defensive porcupines like tektite.

Prairie dogs prefer chalcopyrite and swift rabbits use bloodstone or coral. The dexterous raccoon loves obsidian and gypsum, whereas rams prefer feldspar and petrified wood. Rats vibrate to howlite and zoisite, and peaceful sheep also like howlite. Respectable skunks resonate with blue chalcedony, but active squirrels prefer tree agate or snakeskin agate. Snakes also vibrate to snakeskin agate, and the powerful tiger prefers a tiger's eye.

Sly weasels love indigo agate and labradorite, whereas the guardian wolf vibrates best with ammonite, pyrite, and kambaba jasper. Black and white thinking zebras prefer onyx or zebra jasper.

Combine any of the matching crystals to your animal spirit during meditation to amplify the connection. You can hold them in your hands while you sit in the easy yoga pose, and you can place one behind your tailbone to link your sacral chakra to the ground. Place another stone on your core chakra over the stomach and another on the heart chakra if you're lying down. Add two more stones to make it even more powerful. Rest one stone on your throat chakra and another on your third eye chakra between your eyebrows. Now, all you need to do is learn to listen to your spirit animal. It doesn't help if you aren't tuned in to the same frequency because that won't strengthen the bonds.

3

WHAT DOES IT MEAN WHEN SPIRIT ANIMALS APPEAR TO YOU?

Most often, we're closed to the spirit world until we intentionally open it. This doesn't stop the spirit world and all its guides from trying to connect with us, even when we're unaware. Spirit animals appear to us in multiple ways, and all we need to do is listen to their calls. This will allow them to guide and teach us.

HOW THEY APPEAR

Spirit animals have two main reasons for appearing to us. Our guides will teach us lessons about life and nature while empowering our character strengths or developing them organically. Remember that even while dormant, they never leave your side. They watch over you and will step in when something isn't right in your life. Sometimes, you need to learn a lesson about being compassionate, and other times you face emotional problems the animal spirit can help with.

Allowing your spirit animal to bond with you will improve your physical and mental health while enhancing your knowledge about the earth (Ruhl, 2016). The wiser you grow about the life force of nature, the closer you become to being one with it. Never give up if your animal hasn't appeared yet. Instead, look for signs in your dreams, daily life, and preferences. Spirit animals can appear subtly, but communication with us is strongest during our lower consciousness.

That's why many of them appear first in our dreams. Ask yourself a few questions to become aware of any spirit animals trying to communicate with you.

- Have you ever felt strongly drawn to an animal for unexplainable reasons?
- Have any animals randomly appeared in your life recently?
- Do you have more interest than you can explain in a certain animal when you see them grouped?
- Are you terrified or intrigued by any particular animal?
- Have animals attacked you recently?

- Are there frequent signs that relate to an animal or their crystals?
- Are your dreams filled with recurring appearances of certain animals?
- Do you find specific animal paintings and drawings attractive?

There are so many ways they can make themselves known, even by attacking you. Normally, an aggressive appearance will be to get your attention quickly or to warn you about something. For example, being attacked by ants could indicate that you've procrastinated too long on a project at work. You need to get back to it before it resonates with negative energy throughout your life.

Spirit animals love being bonded deeply to you, but most of them will appear for a good reason. Their first purpose is to teach you lessons and you won't be successful, happy, or healthy if you refuse to listen. You know what I mean if you're an avid meditator. Listening isn't always through sounds either. Watch their actions because they could be warnings. A spirit animal could also positively guide you through actions.

A bear might appear suddenly to make you aware of opportunities. Remember that bears are determined to reach their desires and won't compromise their values along the way.

Therefore, a bear chasing you through the woods could indicate that they're trying to direct you to an opportunity at work or home. Their persistence might make them seem aggressive but the meaning of this dream isn't negative.

Once you know how your spirit animal is appearing to you, keep an eye out for more signs, and try to connect with them through meditation. Keep a journal of your encounters and revisit Chapter One to reread the characteristics of your animals. Are they trying to prompt you to take action or be more aggressive to get the promotion you want? Is the snake reminding you how to heal from past trauma by wrapping itself around you in dreams?

Every animal's characteristics will help you translate the messages you receive from them. Pay attention to the way they use their strengths and the environment you're in. Sometimes, they can use the environment to help you understand because most spirit animals won't communicate verbally. They can connect with you in four ways in dreams or an awakened state (Laing, 2018).

Visual messages are the simplest to translate. The raccoon staring at you is trying to show you that you must pay attention because something is coming your way. This animal is famous for being dexterous and adaptable, so it means that you must also be ready to adapt to the opportunity coming. It could also mean that you must be flexible to change if something goes wrong. Life lessons are opportunistic and sometimes show warning signs.

Your animal spirit might also use auditory communication. You can hear the sounds of rats scurrying and your awareness of the potential future is heightened. Are the rats scurrying because they're afraid? Something is about to happen in your life and you might need to be cunning or stealthy to avoid trouble.

The third kind of communication is kinesthetic when you feel the presence of your animal spirit. You have to pay attention to the emotions while you feel them. Feeling a sloth might make you feel weary and maybe you need to slow down and think about what you're doing. We can only translate our emotions when an animal speaks to us kinesthetically. This is also known as having intuition.

The final communication type is cognitive. Knowing thoughtfully that your animal is around is often called insight or inspiration. You were spontaneously creative and surprised yourself. This could mean that the red fox is communicating with you on a subconscious level.

TRANSLATIONS

Every visit from your animal spirit will indicate a different lesson or guidance. It will depend on the animal, type of communication, or the message you instinctively perceive that aligns with current circumstances in your life. I'm going to share some examples with you so that you know how to translate the animal spirit's characteristics into your visualizations or interactions when you dream, meditate, or encounter the beast by chance.

Let's start with a fun one. You've been dreaming of a baboon picking fleas off its partner's back. Baboons are divine and offer guidance into the spirit world, but they're also keen on relationships with their loved ones and are rather sexually promiscuous. Compare this to your current relationship. Are you and your partner experiencing problems? Maybe you haven't been as intimate as you once were. The baboon is teaching you to pay more attention to your partner, including intimacy.

Let's look into a dream where you're riding a camel across the desert. How do you feel as you ride over the dunes? The emotions you experience might matter in this dream. Now, look at your life and determine whether any struggles make you feel restricted, anxious, or negative. Also, determine whether the camel is carrying you to an oasis or not. Camels are capable of enduring some of the worst obstacles. Allow the camel to show you that it always reaches the oasis. Don't you see an oasis in your dream? This would indicate that you need to identify people or choices that are holding you back from overcoming your fears. There might be someone whose negative energy is rubbing off on you. Spirit animals will often warn us against negative energies.

Another example might be when you dream of a wolf growling at you. You want to walk down a certain path in the woods and the wolf stands in your way. This dream is easy to translate because you need to determine what new path you can switch to in life. Maybe you want to start a job at a new company or move away from your current field. The wolf is warning you that this isn't the best option for you right now. They're telling you to stop and remain where you are for now because there's danger ahead. Listen to your animal spirit because it's protecting you.

You might be dreaming of a deer on your lawn. You might even see one in real life, depending on where you live. Deer are there to guide you gently when emotions become overwhelming. What is the deer doing? You might see the deer eating your grass instead of feeding off the nutritious vegetation in the woods beyond your yard. Translating this is simple again. The deer is an emotional regulator and it's trying to tell you that better days are coming. You can't always hope for the greener grass next door because it only looks brighter. It might be even more tainted than yours. The deer is telling you to be patient and understand that your grass might only be dry for now.

ANIMAL MEDITATION PART ONE

Finally, dreaming of a jaguar hunting its prey could also be a good omen. Jaguars are multitaskers and they're determined to get what they want. They're also disciplined and don't allow chaos to deter them from their kill. Be like your jaguar spirit and see what needs persistent and strategic pursuit in your life. You aren't the prey in this dream unless you're afraid of the jaguar. Allow your emotions to confirm that you feel the adrenaline as the jaguar leaps for the kill.

Our animal spirits are easy to understand if we know what their traits are. Continue to refer back to the guide in Chapter One to determine what the lesson is. Now, it's time to meditate on and connect with these amazing creatures. I'll include four sessions that can help with certain problems you're facing or goals you're trying to obtain. Go through it once and customize each one to suit your spirit animal once you know which one it is.

4

GUIDED SESSION FOR INITIAL CONNECTION

We all have animal spirits walking with us but we need to find a way to connect with them. We can't do this unless we welcome them into our life. This session is dedicated to helping you connect with the spirit animals that have been trying to communicate with you. Once connected, you'll learn more about them and be able to use their strengths to advance in a life you want.

The best position for the initial connection is to use an easy yoga pose, sitting with an erect spine and crossed legs. Allow your palms to face upwards while your hands rest on your knees. You're welcome to use any crystals that connect to certain animals you suspect are already near.

CALLING YOUR SPIRIT ANIMAL

Find a comfortable place to ground yourself in your meditation position and welcome my voice to guide you along this journey. Keep your eyes open for now and find something you can focus on while you take a deep breath. It might be a spot on the wall or a pretty flower in the garden.

Feel your body and how the sensations are circling around you now as you take another deep even breath through your nose. Follow the air into your lungs and let it sit here for a moment. Don't take your eyes off the focal point as you exhale slowly between your lips.

Allow your thoughts to be themselves now. Your greatest intention for connection is to be no one but yourself. Take another deep breath and keep your eyes fixed on the spot. Who are you inside and what are your dreams in life? Have you experienced something that made you stop and think, "wow, I'm good at this"?

It doesn't matter what your strengths are, as long as you identify five of your greatest attributes. Take another breath and never stop the even flow of air into your body and out your mouth. Every droplet of air is being processed in your deepest core before it exits, taking every tension away from your mind and body.

Keep breathing for a few more moments as you welcome your true self to the front. Your eyes fall shut slowly as you allow the thoughts to open emotions. Your true feelings are present in your body and you can still see your focal point through your eyelids. It's imprinted a memory to guide you through this session.

Determine what your emotions can tell you about your thoughts as you continue to draw deep breaths and release them slowly. Your heart is pumping slower now and you're coming closer to reaching an epiphany. Who are you and what do you desire? Is there an anxious emotion inside of you?

Do you enjoy fear or would you like to be more resilient against it? Maybe your thoughts are hovering over a characteristic you want to change. Fear isn't the only one. Take another deep breath and never stop regulating your even cycles. The air goes into your lungs and exits slowly from your mouth.

Allow every emotion to drive the true intention behind your desires. Do you wish to be more creative? Has curiosity always been in your mind but you haven't allowed it to surface? All your thoughts and emotions are welcome in this space you're creating internally, whether they're good or bad.

ANIMAL MEDITATION PART ONE

You want to guide your intention to either let go of unwanted emotions or to build the character traits you would like to grow even stronger. You have the strength inside of you. You simply need to keep searching while you welcome the sensations that accompany it. Your breathing is becoming even slower now and your heart is taking a brief stroll along a path of relaxation.

Have you lost contact with your focal spot yet or are you still watching it? Your thoughts and emotions are ready now and you can pay attention to the spot again. Use an inner voice or say it out loud if it feels more powerful this way. Use mantras to confirm what you've learned so that you can accept the unwanted and desired traits to set your intention now.

Repeat your mantras while you keep looking at the image that seems to be changing slowly. It's coming closer to you and it's gaining new form as you repeat those positive and affirming mantras. Use the universal mantra to end the repetition of your own.

"I'm ready for whatever forms in front of me."

Welcome the image with this final mantra and allow the dot to form an animal. What animal do you see? Does it have fur or can you see the spikes of a porcupine? The image remains blurry because you need to be sure that you're receptive for the spirit animal to connect with you. You know what your deepest desires are and what you want to be removed.

Don't be afraid to speak to the animal. Welcome it nearer to you by calling upon it. You can use its name if you can determine what it is now. Let this incredible creature know that you're receptive. Call it to your vision and assure it that you're ready to let go of what needs to be erased.

Use mantras again as you keep your focus sharply on the image drawing nearer.

"I'm waiting for you to bestow the gift of your sight on me. Reveal what you want me to see and guide me to move away from the things I don't want to see anymore."

Be sincere and only call the animal if you mean to. Wait in this silent space until the animal takes a clearer form. What animal do you see? How does it make you feel when it comes even closer? Pay attention to the emotions changing inside of you as the animal takes the final steps to get to you.

Share positive and warm energy with the creature as you let it know that you're happy to see it. Thank the animal for choosing to connect with you. Focus on every sensory interaction between you and this creature. Smell its presence and listen to the sounds beneath its breath.

Allow your spirit animal to approach you as you reach out and touch its soft fur. How beautiful is this animal up close? Spend a few moments in this glorious space where it's just your true self and the beast in front of you. You don't need to do anything more once you've touched the animal.

Allow yourself to be comfortable in its spiritual essence before you return to your meditation space. You can shift your attention to your breath again when you want to return from this meeting. Count 10 breaths in and out slowly as the image grows more distant from you again.

The image has become the original focal spot when you slowly open your eyes on the tenth exhale. Take some time to reflect on how your thoughts and emotions have been accepted before you leave your peaceful position. This includes the new excitement after meeting your animal spirit.

5

GUIDED SESSION FOR SELF-IMPROVEMENT

Self-growth is something we can all harness through our spirit animals. This session will be dedicated to finding the adventurous, curious, and empowering part of yourself by tapping into your animal totem. Use any animal you possess, for this exercise I'll be using a horse. It will be better if you use agate crystals. Sit in an easy yoga position with your hands resting on your knees and your spine erect. You want to feel freedom and empowerment. Place one agate at your sacral region that connects to the ground and hold two more in your upward-facing palms.

HORSING SPIRITS

Follow the tone of my voice as I guide you on a journey that brings you closer to your empowerment. Pay attention to

ANIMAL MEDITATION PART ONE

the stones in your hands as you take a deep breath for three seconds. Hold the air and feel the sensation of freshness in your lungs before pressing it out gently for another three seconds.

Close your eyes and take another three-second breath as you follow its treacle down your throat. Clean air is gently massaging your diaphragm as you hold it for a second. Now, purse your lips and push it out gently for three seconds. I want you to use the three-second rule for every ounce of air that moves in or out.

Take another breath as you set your intention for the session. Think about the improvements you yearn for as the air tickles your insides. Press it out gently through your mouth again as your spine straightens even further. You want the breath to travel deeper while your thoughts focus on your intentions.

Try to pull the air gently into your stomach and core muscles. Don't force it harshly, but just allow it to go deeper. Your mind is shuffling through the improvement options when you reach an epiphany. Press the air out gently as you allow your thoughts to speak to you. Draw another slow and steady breath while you think about growth.

Growth comes from a simple trait you can use. Allow the breath to reach your core again as you feel more and more relaxed. You can connect to a spirit that will teach you self-improvement. Any creature with curiosity and adventurous spirit will open your dreams up to reality.

You aren't ready just yet. Keep breathing while you focus on your muscles now. You can feel your feet grow lighter as you take another breath. Push it out slowly as you feel the tension release from your legs. Your core is tight and you need another deep controlled breath to reach it.

Welcome the air as you know your intentions. You are eager to become weightless enough to bond with your animal spirit. Feel the air pass into your core as it collects the tightness and hold it for a moment. Press the air out slowly and feel how the tension relieves from the core.

Focus strongly on your upper body and allow your breath to guide your muscles into a relaxed state. Take as long as you need to unknot every muscle without bending your spine. You can feel the warm energy in every breath you draw through your throat. Don't stop breathing and scan your muscles for more tension.

Your spirit animal is waiting for you. Allow your heart to release the energy around it by pushing air out gently. Can you feel how it has slowed down gradually? The thumps have turned into gentle, slow beats now. Take another breath as you fixate on blending your intention with your

ANIMAL MEDITATION PART ONE

heart chakra. You can feel the blue warmth surrounding it as you exhale.

Relax your throat with another breath before you move your focus to the temple of your mind. Allow your third eye to relax as the air circulates here. Your blood is carrying the cleanest of air and your third eye submits. Your spiritual being resides just above the third eye. Take another breath and hold it until you feel connected to something larger.

Release the air as your weight shifts deeply into the ground beneath you. Your spine is connecting the spirit world to the earth and you can open your third eye now. Continue breathing as you call for your spirit animal with your inner voice. Call the horse and feel how your spirit embodies its muscular frame.

Don't rush the bondage and take it slow as you allow the horse to overtake your spiritual connection. When you're ready at your own time, your body feels different. You can feel the power in your muscles that were never there before. Your hooves are planted firmly into the ground but you can feel the freedom around you.

Don't be shy and allow yourself to start galloping slowly. The horse is welcoming you to its embodiment. You must welcome the bondage between you now. Give into its power as you take the first step forward. You've become one with the nature of this incredibly strong beast and it allows you to control its energy now.

Start speeding up as those trotters hit the ground hard with every gallop. Have you ever felt so free in your life? Suddenly, the horse shares its adventurous spirit with you. You can feel curiosity and a deep urge for adventure in every muscle. You're overwhelmed by its nature. Don't be scared of your spirit animal.

Flow with its energy as you're sprinting now. You need more in life and the horse's embodiment allows you to run for it. Use every powerful muscle to get closer to the image ahead, whatever it might be. Feel the excitement that curiosity brings. Feel the freedom of adventure in your energy.

A picture is forming in front of your inner vision and you speed up even more. Nothing can stop the movements of this powerful beast now. What comes after the image clears is up to you. Allow the horse to move at the speed of light as you keep connecting back to the ground with your hooves.

Kick yourself forward and allow every emotion to engulf you. You can run towards your empowerment and growth as long as you like, but slow the horse down when you're ready to return. Do it gradually as you feel your essence separating from the horse now. Focus on your breathing as

ANIMAL MEDITATION PART ONE

you reflect on the feeling of adventurous freedom and curiosity.

All of that was combined with a powerful force that drives you to your improvements. Start counting to three with every exhale again. Pull fresh air into your stomach as you count to three once more. Do this for a few cycles as each brings you one step closer to your physical presence again.

You slowly feel yourself separate from the ground and the spirit realm as you take another breath. Press it out slowly as you open your eyes. Now, sit there and scan your body for all the new sensations you feel. Reflect on the changes you feel emotionally and physically. Allow your mind to absorb every sensation before you move again.

Feel free to allow your spirit animal to bond with you anytime you want to feel the power that moves you towards ambitions and self-growth.

6

GUIDED SESSION TO HEAL FROM PAST TRAUMA

Nobody wants to experience trauma or emotional unrest that stops us from fulfilling our full potential, but most of us have sadly succumbed to it at some point in life, and now we carry the burden with us. This session is dedicated to healing from past trauma and using your spirit animal to dissipate emotional problems. It can also work for physical ailments because I'm going to use a snake, but you can use any spirit guide that rejuvenates, heals, or renews.

I recommend that you lie down for this one and use seven pieces of snakeskin agate. Place them along your chakra energy centers. One can be under your tailbone, the second must lie in your pelvis, the third on your navel, and the fourth one lies on your heart. The fifth stone is placed on your throat, the sixth stone on your forehead, and the final piece must be above your head because the spiritual realm resides above you.

SLITHERING REJUVENATION

Close your eyes and listen to the calm tone of my voice as you start breathing slowly and evenly. Count to three on every inhale and hold the breath for a second before pushing it out gently for another three seconds. Always allow your breaths to become even. You can do it slowly if your breathing is still rapid.

Slow and steady intakes and exits are advised as you keep focusing on my voice. Feel the air pass through your throat as your stone permeates with gentle energy. It passes the heart and lights up your energy center keeping the heart safe. Push the air out gently and take another deeper, slower breath.

Follow this one deeper into your core as you feel the stones calming you down. Your breath grows deeper and slower with each inhale and your core stone is gathering energy now. Feel your muscles relax as every stone vibrates along your body, right down to your sacral stone under the tailbone.

Continue passing clean air into your body and pushing unwanted, unpleasant air out for three seconds. Your body is growing lighter at a slow pace. Listen to your heart as its rhythm slows down gradually. Take another deep breath into your core and allow your muscles to conform to the calming energy of each stone.

Gently shift your focus to your mind as you continue breathing evenly. Your mind is stressed. It's feeling uncalm and the energy surrounding it is warm. You want to cool the energy down. Set your intention for the energy shift and allow your mind to experience a new, long-missed sensation.

It will take some work but I want you to scan the rest of your body now and notice if there are tense places. It's the mind that controls the tension. Just focus on them for a while as you keep breathing evenly. Focus on how close these tense muscles are to each stone you've carefully placed over your energy centers.

Every stone is slightly warmer now and you can feel the tightness surrounding the core and heart centers. You might also feel tightness around the sacral center as you simply notice them. You're reflecting on how you feel right now before you allow your hands to rise and make gentle contact with your skin.

Your arms are more relaxed even if there's tightness in them. Your body has comfortably grounded into the surface beneath you as you draw another gentle and steady breath. Pay attention to your energy centers as your fingertips touch your stomach's skin gently. You can feel slight friction between the skin and fingers.

Gently run your fingers across your stomach and follow the friction in the touch. You need to take a few more breaths and open your spiritual mind. Move your focus from the friction for now and follow your breath into your mind again. You can feel the energy surrounding the third eye energy center.

Pay close attention to it as you keep breathing evenly and notice how the energy is growing stronger. The stone on your forehead is magnifying the energy and concentrating it to the third eye region. Take another deeper breath and hold the air as your mind opens slowly. Your spiritual essence has been welcomed into your grounded presence.

Open the third eye and allow the sensory stimuli to attract your attention back to the friction between your fingers and skin now. But wait, it feels different now. The warm energy is being countered by a spiritual rejuvenator. You can feel the slithering and cold presence move across your skin as you intentionally move your fingers around.

A bonded snake has heard your call for spiritual help. Welcome the creature as it means you no harm. Feel its belly slither over your core muscles. There's an odd sensation when it passes over the core of your stomach. The snake is pulling the warmer, unwanted energy into its cold belly.

Don't fear for the snake either. These creatures were built to withstand the negative energy it draws out of your skin. It stores the energy which is poisonous to you, but not to them. You feel weird comfort as the snake continues to slither around your stomach and moves slowly towards your sacral region.

It heads downwards and comes back towards your heart chakra. The snake can sense the tension in your heart and wants you to guide it over the poisonous energy to remove it. Use your fingertips to show the snake where it hurts. It will move everywhere you run your fingers gently.

The cold feeling from its belly is absorbing the unwanted energy in your chosen directions. The snake nears your heart and you pay close attention to how the poison leaves your body through its belly. The snake knows where the source of this poison is and you can simply give it permission to follow its instincts now.

It slithers over your throat and onto your face. It never stops you from drawing even breaths, but it rests on your forehead. The snake intends to absorb all the negative energy and traumatic pain from the mind. Leave it be as it rests

ANIMAL MEDITATION PART ONE

there and just pay attention to the mystical essence that draws the pain from your body.

Stay in this position until you feel like the snake has consumed enough poison for now. Once you're feeling better, slowly focus on your breath again. Continue running your fingers across your stomach as you count five breath cycles. It's a slow return but you can start feeling the friction between your fingers and skin again.

The snake is gone for now but its spiritual essence has left a connection to your mind. After your five breaths, you'll feel more present in your own essence again. Rest your arms next to you and scan your stones once more. The temperature and essence of each snakeskin agate are different. They're cooler and calmer now.

Reflect on the way your body feels free from pain at this moment. The snake can come back anytime you want them to, but for now, just be with your ultimately calm body. Open your eyes after taking one more deep breath and pay attention to how great you feel. Your intention was reached and you became one with the healing snake.

7

GUIDED SESSION FOR A DEEPER PURPOSE

Often, all we need is some guidance and clarity. This session will focus on spirit animal meditation that offers you just that. I'll use the mighty wolf that opens our spirituality, but you can use any animal that offers guidance. You'll sit in the easy yoga pose once again with your hands rested subtly on your knees. Choose any stone that works with the wolf and place it on your crown because you want to open your spiritual essence.

A WELCOMED COMPANION

Listen to the sound of my voice as you feel your sacral region against the ground beneath you. Just pay close attention to the sensation of the earth while you count your breaths in and out slowly. Welcome the air into your body with a deeper inhale and keep it in your lungs for a while. Take the air into your nose and press it gently out of your pursed lips while reaching the count of three.

Keep breathing gently and slowly as you notice the stone placed on the crown of your head. You need to gradually allow the stone to open your pathway to the spiritual world. Your body rises subtly with every intake of breath and it falls gently back into the earth as you push the air out again. Start thinking about the intention you'd like to set when you welcome your companion.

Take another deep breath in as you consider all the possible intentions a spiritual guide can bring to you. Consider your dreams and aspirations as you exhale slowly. Take another breath in and realize what your intention is. You might want guidance in a life that seems to have no direction. You may want a guide to deepen your spiritual connection.

Take another five breaths in and out as you pinpoint the desires you want from a companion. Now, I want you to relax your muscles by scanning your body for any tightness again. Allow the cool air to enter your body and remove tension from areas that don't feel relaxed enough. Do it slowly as you start with your feet. Pull your muscles tight and release them if it helps.

Move up to your legs and pull those muscles tight before abruptly letting them go. You must let go of every tightness in your butt before moving to your stomach. Breathe deeply as you clear the tension from your core and move to your chest. Take a deeper breath and keep it in your lungs as long as you can. It will collect the tightness that lingers in your chest area.

Focus on your hands and arms now by pulling your muscles a little tighter and releasing them when you exhale. Open your jaw wide and shut it after pressing the air out to release the tension in your lower face. Keep breathing gently as you raise your eyebrows to the heavens. Hold them for a second and release them quickly. Your body feels lighter, more relaxed, and just about ready.

Allow your third eye to start stirring as you feel the crown above your head open up. It feels like a stream of white, calm energy flowing into your mind from above. Use your inner eyes to watch as the brightness of your energy floods into your crown. You've activated the stone above your crown and chosen to welcome the energy into your being. Stay in this state for a moment and reflect on the beautiful purity streaming into you.

I want you to feel the cold embrace against your nose. There's a cool touch that has some wetness involved. This feeling doesn't frighten you. In fact, it welcomes and urges you to open your third eye now. Your inner vision opens slowly as the image in front of you starts to form. You can make sense of the woods surrounding you as the image of a majestic wolf stands right in front of you.

There's a strange calmness about you as the wolf steps forward and embraces your nose with his wet snout again. Allow the blurry image to clarify perfectly before you interact with this incredible creature. Listen to the sounds of the birds in the trees and the water running nearby as you focus on the wolf. The wolf spirit shares a connection with you as you notice the white energy flowing from its head into your stream.

Allow yourself to rise in your image as soon as the wolf is clear. This amazing creature's demeanor is welcoming, warm, and friendly. It nudges you against the nose one more time before you realize that it wants you to follow it. Permit your spirit to follow the guidance of this wolf. Open your mind to allowing the wolf to choose your next step.

Multiple pathways are running through this incredibly green forest as the trees stand tall over you. The trees are protective and the wolf is now standing at a crossroads between the trees. You're unsure of where each path leads, but your curiosity is peaking. Join the wolf at the crossroads and stand there for a moment.

The wolf is waiting for your permission to go ahead. Just take in the beauty of your surroundings as the wolf stands strong at your side. You can smell things you've never experienced before. Immerse yourself in the sensory experience of these woods and shift your attention to the powerful beast beside you.

Communicate with the beast by letting it know that you're ready. You'll follow it anywhere it leads you. Suddenly, the wolf guide disappears down the center pathway. You stand there for a while, reflecting on the choice of the wolf. Your heart feels lighter, happier, and accepting of the wolf's decision. Reflect on this acceptance for a moment before taking a step down the pathway.

Just beyond the trees, your inner sight catches the wolf again. It's continuing down this path and suddenly, you're overwhelmed with the incredible picture in front of you. You've never seen or felt anything like this before. There's a massive waterfall in the clearing of the trees and you can feel an extreme urge to reach it. Go ahead and follow your wolf as you near the waterfall.

You can hear the water crashing down on the rocks beneath but the sight is something you could never have imagined. There's a strange white aura surrounding the water. It's not quite the type you normally see. It looks similar to the white

ANIMAL MEDITATION PART ONE

energy flowing into your crown. Stroll to the water's edge and seat yourself in the ground.

Allow the ground to become part of you as you spend as much time in your spiritual haven as you wish. The wolf sits beside you and you can feel its fur touching your skin as the pure energy floods into your crown. You feel calmer and more confident than you've ever been before. You get to share this scene with your spirit guide as long as you want to remain.

Anytime you feel ready to leave your spiritual realm, allow your breath to gradually bring you back. Let go of the image and allow it to blur again as you grow more distant with every breath you take. Take another five breaths in and out as you count to three on each cycle and allow your third eye to shut for now again.

You're back on your meditation spot and you can slowly open your eyes. Spend a few minutes reflecting on how this meditation made you feel. How did you feel after welcoming your companion into your life? Allow every emotion to find its corner in your mind. Allow every revelation to help you accept that you're on the right path now.

CONCLUSION

Walking with your animal spirit is a journey like no other. You've been held back until now, always wanting more but not knowing how to get it. We all face decisions in our lives and more often than not, we choose the wrong option. Have you been in the same industry for too many years? How long will you continue to wait until your life erupts into an endless source of momentous energy? Too many people are miserable under the surface because they can't figure out what's missing. Failing to connect with your deeper spiritual self is like trying to bat blindly for the team that's one run away from winning.

You might've suffered unimaginable pains that prevented you from being successful. These pains could be mental, emotional, or physical. However, now you know how to overcome any obstacle even if you already practice holistic

CONCLUSION

healing and mindfulness. You don't need to be some guru or chieftain to call upon the souls deeply connected to yours. Your well being is just as important to your spirit animal as their own. Each creature walks this earth and waits for the calls from their human soulmate. Chances are they've been at your side all along and all you had to do was make contact.

Everything becomes possible when you allow your guiding animal to connect you to the spirit realm. You have everything you need inside of you and they can help you bring it out. I could never have imagined this life if I ignored the visitations and obvious signs from my guides. They walked with me and helped overcome unthinkable heights. Animals aren't meant to only be revered or seen as beautiful. Their souls are just as complex as our own. You must now use the information you've learned to find yours. Call them into your life so they can entrust you with the gifts you are meant to have.

Reaching the required state of consciousness is covered in the guided sessions you just read. Use the crystals to enhance communication and store the energy your spirit animal shares. Sometimes, we need a little positive energy to face what each day brings. Try to connect with your animals often and keep your eyes open for the signs and warnings they bring. The spirit realm knows what happens next in life, knows where you need to step so as to prevent disaster.

CONCLUSION

Our spirituality is what makes us human; it empowers us to be who we need to be.

Never let doubt flood your mind again. You know which animal spirits will give you the strength to pursue your goals. Harnessing the power of spirit guides might even help you surpass all expectations. Don't allow anything to stand in the way of your ultimate desires again. You have everything you need to intertwine your soul with your spirit animal; so go out and be the person you were meant to be.

REFERENCES

Beauchesne, M. (2018, September 19). *The origination of the spirit animal.* Kheops International. https://kheopsinternational.com/blog/origination-of-the-spirit-animal/

Gaia Staff. (2014, August 22). *3 spirit animal meditations: Contact your animal guide.* Gaia. https://www.gaia.com/article/3-spirit-animal-meditations?render=details-v4

Harris, E. (2019, October 28). *How to find your spirit animal.* Spirit Animal Info. https://www.spiritanimal.info/how-to-find-spirit-animal/

Laing, K. (2018, May 7). *Understanding animal spirit guides.* Karin Laing. https://karinlaing.com/blog/2018/05/07/understanding-animal-spirit-guides/

REFERENCES

Legends of America. (2019a, May 12). *Native American totem animals & their meanings.* Legends of America. https://www.legendsofamerica.com/na-totems/

Mildon, E. (2017, May 17). *What's your spirit animal? Here's exactly how to find out.* Mind Body Green. https://www.mindbodygreen.com/articles/how-to-find-your-spirit-animal

Ruhl, B. (2016, August 18). *Animal spirits — your guide to a better life.* Medium. https://medium.com/@barbruhl/animal-spirits-your-guide-to-a-better-life-5cab0eedbcb0

Sage Goddess. (2017, May 2). *Crystal guide for spirit animals.* Sage Goddess. https://www.sagegoddess.com/crystals/crystal-guide-for-spirit-animals/

Spirit Animal Totems. (2019b, October 11). *Animal symbolism; your animal guide.* Spirit Animal Totems. https://www.spirit-animals.com/

Spirit Walk Ministry. (n.d.). *Land animal spirits.* Spirit Walk Ministry. https://www.spiritwalkministry.com/spirit_guides/land_animal_spirits

Wolf Sister. (2016, July 19). *How to work with your spirit animal: A total guide.* Numinous. https://www.the-numinous.com/2016/07/19/work-with-your-spirit-animal/

www.ingramcontent.com/pod-product-compliance
Lightning Source LLC
Chambersburg PA
CBHW071506070526
44578CB00001B/457